UTAH

GRAPHIC·ARTS™·BOOKS

INTRODUCTION

My first excursion to Utah was on a cold and stormy November day in 1977. I drove south from my seasonal park ranger job in Yellowstone in a drafty 1958 Chevrolet Apache pickup. Hour after hour of heavy snow left me road weary and ready to winter camp. When I arrived at Bryce Canyon, a makeshift sign proclaimed "campgrounds closed due to deep snow, overnight camping allowed in Visitor Center parking lot."

I was the only camper and after setting up, I strapped on my cross-country skis and broke trail to the Bryce rim. What a sight to behold! Snow-laden clouds raced over the Paunsaugunt Plateau. Occasional breaks allowed moonlight to illuminate a surreal landscape of swirling snow and legions of strange limestone spires. I thought to myself, *This place is incredible, I'd sure like to spend the winter here.*

The next morning I trundled into the Visitor Center, inquired about winter work, and to my delight found the park needing an employee to break trails, shovel roofs, staff the Visitor Center, and rout wooden signs. I signed up on the spot. Bryce ended up having the snowiest winter on record and I came to intimately know the park in glorious winter wraps.

On my days off, I cross-country skied and found snow-stranded cattle for local ranchers. Families with last names of Pollock, Shakespeare, and Syrett shared knowledge of the land gleaned from generations dating from when Brigham Young sent the Saints south to populate Utah's far reaches. I learned of dinosaur tracks deep within Hackberry Canyon, seldom-visited Sam Pollock Arch in Lower Death Valley, and eerie narrows of Bull Valley Gorge. And in my excitement to visit

these places, I also learned Kane County's diamond signs proclaiming "Impassable When Wet" spoke truthfully of gumbo-thick mud that entrapped vehicles, even 1958 Apache pickups, that dared cross blue hills of bentonite clay when snow melted.

In the thirty years since that wonderful Bryce Canyon winter, Utah continually beckons as a favorite place to stretch my hiking legs, shoulder a pack, and explore. The Beehive State's variety of landscapes makes Utah an easy place to photograph; everywhere breathtaking scenery awaits capture!

Utah's diversity astounds. In the north, the Wasatch Range and Uinta Mountains provide some of the Rocky Mountains' most stunning alpine scenery. To the west stretch Great Salt Lake and Utah Lake, beautiful remnants of a vast inland sea. Beyond their sparkling waters marches Basin and Range Country with names befitting the wildness: The Confusion Range, Whirlwind Valley, and Skull Valley. In extreme southwestern Utah, the Mojave Desert appears with Joshua tree forests flanking the Beaver Dam Mountains. But the landscape most people envision when thinking of Utah is the myriad

erosional forms comprising slickrock country. Stretching east from Zion National Park to Flaming Gorge National Recreation Area, Utah's Colorado Plateau holds dramatic sandstone arches, canyons, buttes, and mesas.

It's no wonder that Congress and U.S. presidents created in Utah five national parks: Arches, Bryce Canyon, Canyonlands, Capitol Reef, and Zion; seven national monuments: Cedar Breaks, Dinosaur, Grand Staircase–Escalante, Hovenweep, Natural Bridges, Rainbow Bridge, and Timpanogos Cave; three national recreation areas: Glen Canyon, Flaming Gorge, and Little Sahara; one national historic site: Golden Spike; and eight national forests: Ashley, Caribou-Targhee, Dixie, Fishlake, Manti–La Sal, Sawtooth, Uinta, and Wasatch-Cache. Not to be outdone by the federal government, the citizens of Utah set aside forty-three state parks commemorating Utah's cultural and natural history and favorite recreational areas.

A rich cultural heritage weaves through Utah's stunning landscape. Ancestral Native Americans left exquisitely preserved cliff dwellings and rock art panels. Today, communities of Ute, Southern Paiute, Goshute, Shoshone, and Navajo people live in the state. The first emigrants of Latter-day Saints or Mormons, led by Brigham Young, settled Salt Lake Valley in 1847. By 1869 when driving the golden spike at Promontory completed the transcontinental railroad, 60,000 Mormon settlers had arrived. One hundred fifty years later, more than 2.7 million people of varied ethnic and religious backgrounds, the vast majority living along the Wasatch Front, call Utah home. And an additional 17.5 million people visit Utah annually enjoying the beauty and history.

—FRED HIRSCHMANN

UTAH

FRED HIRSCHMANN

GRAPHIC·ARTS™·BOOKS

▲ Sun dogs or parhelia shine brightly in airborne ice crystals on a subzero morning, Paunsaugunt Plateau above Bryce Canyon.

▶ Dedicated in 1893, the Salt Lake Temple is the best-known temple of the Church of Jesus Christ of Latter-day Saints.

▲ Pale evening primrose
above the Escalante River,
Glen Canyon National
Recreation Area.
▶ Bonneville Salt Flats,
western side of the Great
Salt Lake Desert.

◄ Boat Mesa and the Bryce Amphitheater, Sunset Point, Bryce Canyon National Park.

► Ponderosa pine and Navajo Sandstone walls, Clear Creek Canyon, Zion National Park.

►► Exquisite Ancestral Puebloan pottery, Mesa Verde and Mancos black-on-white ollas, displayed at the Edge of the Cedars State Park Museum in Blanding.

◄ Blowing sand on the
crest of the Sand Hills,
Little Sahara National
Recreation Area.
▲ Rabbitbrush on
the slope of Dutch
Mountain, Toele County.

◄ Dusk descends over Park City, a former silver mining town, turned bustling center for many Wasatch Range ski resorts.

► Blazing alpine sunset reflected in Amethyst Lake, High Uintas Wilderness, Wasatch-Cache National Forest.

NORTHWEST

▲ Details of eroded
gneiss along the shore
of Antelope Island.
► Storm racing across the
Great Salt Lake, Antelope
Island State Park.

▲▲ White pelicans, Bear River Migratory Bird Refuge.

▲▶ Yellow-headed blackbird in tule marsh along the Great Salt Lake.

▲ Mule deer swimming in pond at Fish Springs National Wildlife Refuge.

▶ Kit fox by den, Fish Springs Flat, Juab County.

► Aspen leaves and autumn snow, Fifteen Mile Creek, Deep Creek Range, Goshute Indian Reservation.

◂ Crest of Antelope
Island viewed from
Camera Flats, Antelope
Island State Park.

◄ Abandoned brick home, Grouse Creek established 1875 and now with the moniker "A Place Like No Other," Box Elder County.

▲ Dodge pickup with a few bullet holes marking desert intersection in Tule Valley.

► Goodwin Mercantile, ghost town of Gold Hill, founded 1892 in the Deep Creek Range.

◄ Historic Union Pacific Railroad tracks where the transcontinental railroad was completed in 1869, Golden Spike National Historic Site.

► Working replicas of steam locomotives Jupiter and #119, Golden Spike National Historic Site.

► View from Lincoln Point of Mount Timpanogos rising above Utah Lake and the city of Orem.

◄ Great Salt Lake shoreline at Bridger Bay, Antelope Island State Park.

► Volcano Peak of the Silver Island Mountains rising above Utah swamp fire growing on saline playa.

►► Sunset reflection near mouth of Bear River in Great Salt Lake, Bear River Migratory Bird Refuge.

◄ Moon rising over the Deep Creek Range at sunset, Goshute Indian Reservation.

► Limestone outcrops on Sand Mountain, Little Sahara National Recreation Area, Juab County.

34

► Antelope Island Road winding through Basin and Range topography of Antelope Island.

►► Snowcapped Haystack Peak, 12,020 feet, rising above playa on east side of the Deep Creek Range.

NORTHEAST

▲ Ostler Fork flowing
toward craggy peaks
of the Uinta Mountains,
Wasatch-Cache
National Forest.
► Oddly eroded Uinta
Formation sandstone at
Fantasy Canyon, Devil's
Playground, Uinta Basin.

◄ Classic Vernal Style
Fremont petroglyphs,
McKee Spring, Dinosaur
National Monument.
▲ Large Jurassic dinosaur
track, Hackberry Canyon,
Grand Staircase–Escalante
National Monument.
► Allosaur jaw, vertebrae,
and ribs at the Cleveland-
Lloyd Dinosaur Quarry.

◄ Approaching storm
over archaeologically rich
Nine Mile Canyon and
West Tavaputs Plateau.
▲ Numerous bighorn
sheep Fremont Style
petroglyphs at the
Hunter's Mural, tributary
of Nine Mile Canyon.

◄ Quaking aspen in early spring, West Tavaputs Plateau.
► Pronghorn and mule deer tracks along the sandy shore of freshwater Bear Lake, Bear Lake State Park.

◄ Ostler Peak reflected
in placid water of
Amethyst Lake, High
Uintas Wilderness.
▲ Lodgepole pines with
quaking aspen blooming
in early spring, Ashley
National Forest.

◄ Cottonwoods framing
spire of Goblin City
near Atchees Wash,
Uinta Basin.
► Morning light
illuminating sagebrush
and cottonwoods, Uintah
and Ouray Indian
Reservation.
►► Gatefold: Shore of
Desert Lake at sunrise,
Castle Valley.

◄ Green River meandering through Island Park, Dinosaur National Monument.

► White-tailed prairie dog, Rainbow Park, Dinosaur National Monument.

▼ Mule deer grazing in field near the Strawberry River, Uintah and Ouray Indian Reservation.

◄ White River flowing
through the Uinta Basin
toward the Green River.
▲ Canada geese taking
flight along bank of the
White River.

WASATCH RANGE

▲ Mount Timpanogos
rising above South Fork
of American Fork Canyon,
Uinta National Forest.
► Heartleaf bittercress
along Maybird Creek, Lone
Peak Wilderness, Wasatch-
Cache National Forest.

◄ Ivesia, paintbrush, and yellow columbine blooming below Catherine Pass, Big Cottonwood Canyon.

► Paintbrush, Albion Basin.

►▼ False hellebore, paintbrush, and Richardson geranium.

▼▼ Creamy buckwheat, Wasatch-Cache National Forest.

▼ Mountain sunflower, Little Cottonwood Canyon.

▲ Alpine freestyle extreme skier Dylan Crossman jumping rock outcrop at Alta.

◄ Skiers enjoying two feet of fresh Utah powder in the Wasatch Range.

◄◄ Carving turns through the Greatest Snow on Earth, Little Cottonwood Canyon below Flagstaff Mountain.

► Dylan Crossman negotiates a narrow couloir at Alta Ski Area.

► Sundial Peak reflected in Lake Blanche, Big Cottonwood Canyon, Twin Peaks Wilderness.
►► Mountain sunflower and creamy buckwheat blooming in Albion Basin, Little Cottonwood Canyon.

◄ Sunrise illuminating
Mount Magog rising
above White Pine Lake in
the Bear River Range.
▲ Bicycling Alpine Loop
on the slopes of Mount
Timpanogos in autumn,
Uinta National Forest.

► A lone moose (far right) enters placid water of Lake Lillian surrounded by glacially polished outcrops, Twin Peaks Wilderness, Wasatch-Cache National Forest.

◄ Fall colors along American Fork just east of Timpanogos Cave, Uinta National Forest.

▲ Stewarts Cascades, Mount Timpanogos Wilderness, Uinta National Forest.

►▲ Monkshood blooming along slightly thermal water of Cascade Springs, Uinta National Forest.

► Red Pine Fork cascading from the Wasatch Range, Lone Peak Wilderness, Wasatch-Cache National Forest.

◄ Bigtooth maples in autumn glory, Left Hand Fork Blacksmith Fork Canyon, Bear River Range.
▲ Brilliant red of bigtooth maples in Leatham Hollow, Bear River Range, Wasatch-Cache National Forest.

◄ Engelmann spruce line the Great Western Trail near
Catherine Pass, Wasatch-Cache National Forest.
▲ Autumn gold of quaking aspen, slopes of Mount
Timpanogos, Uinta National Forest.

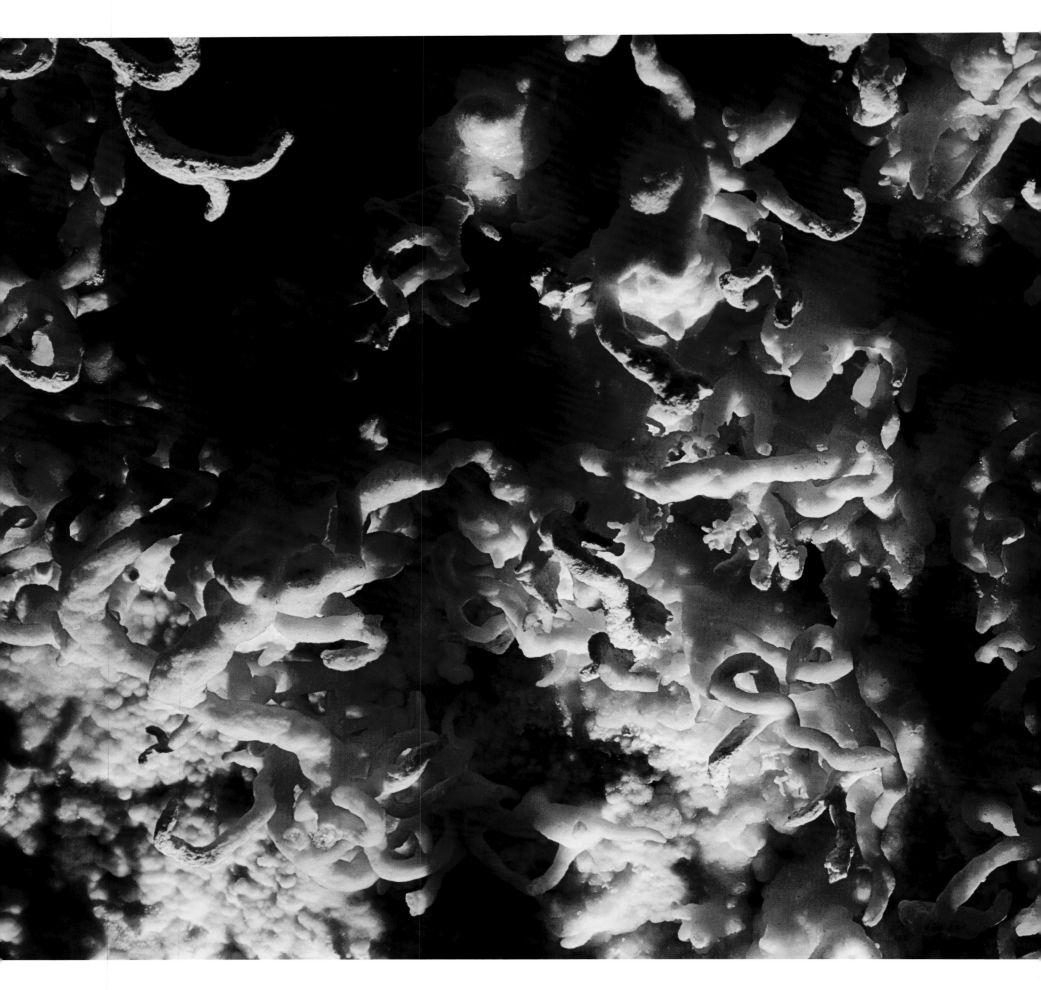

◄ Helictites decorating
ceiling of the Chimes
Chamber, Timpanogos
Cave National Monument.
▲ The Great Heart of
Timpanogos, a calcite
stalactite five and
one-half feet in length,
Timpanogos Cave
National Monument.

◄ McPolin Farm with
barn erected in 1908,
east side of the Wasatch
Range at Park City.
▲ Limber pine covered with
rime, high in the Wasatch
Range at Alta, Wasatch-
Cache National Forest.

◄ Historic Old Main
building on the Utah State
University campus, Logan.
► Logan Utah Temple,
dedicated in 1883 by the
Church of Jesus Christ
of Latter-day Saints.

◄ Manti Utah Temple built
of white oolite limestone,
quarried on the site, and
dedicated in 1888.
► Beehive House and
Lion House, former Salt
Lake residences of
Brigham Young, moved
to Temple Square.

◄ Exquisite interior of the Cathedral of the Madeleine completed in 1918, Salt Lake City.
► Uniquely designed Urban Room of the City Library illuminated at night, Salt Lake City.

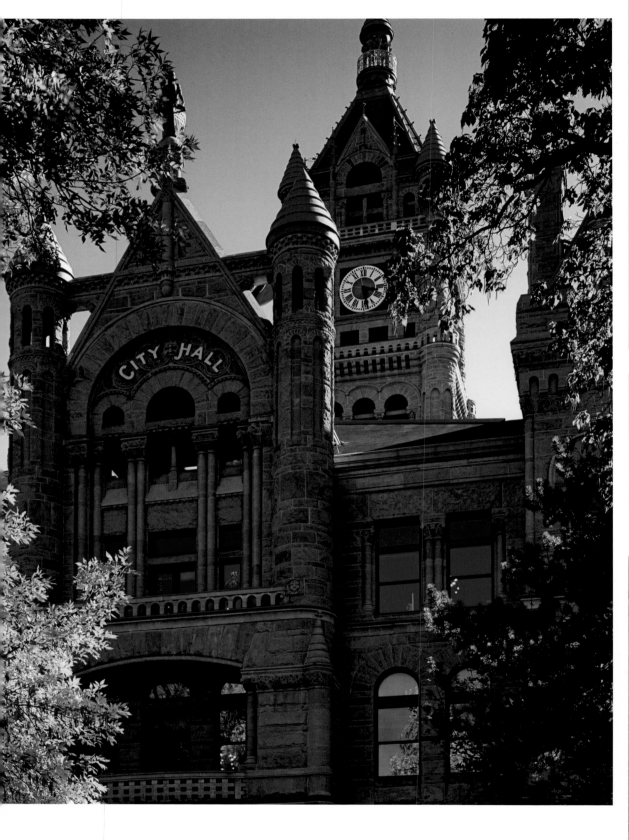

◄ Ornate Salt Lake City and County Building housed Utah's capitol from granting of statehood in 1896 until 1915.

▼ One of the finest homes west of the Mississippi, Salt Lake City's McCune Mansion has been restored to its 1900 grandeur.

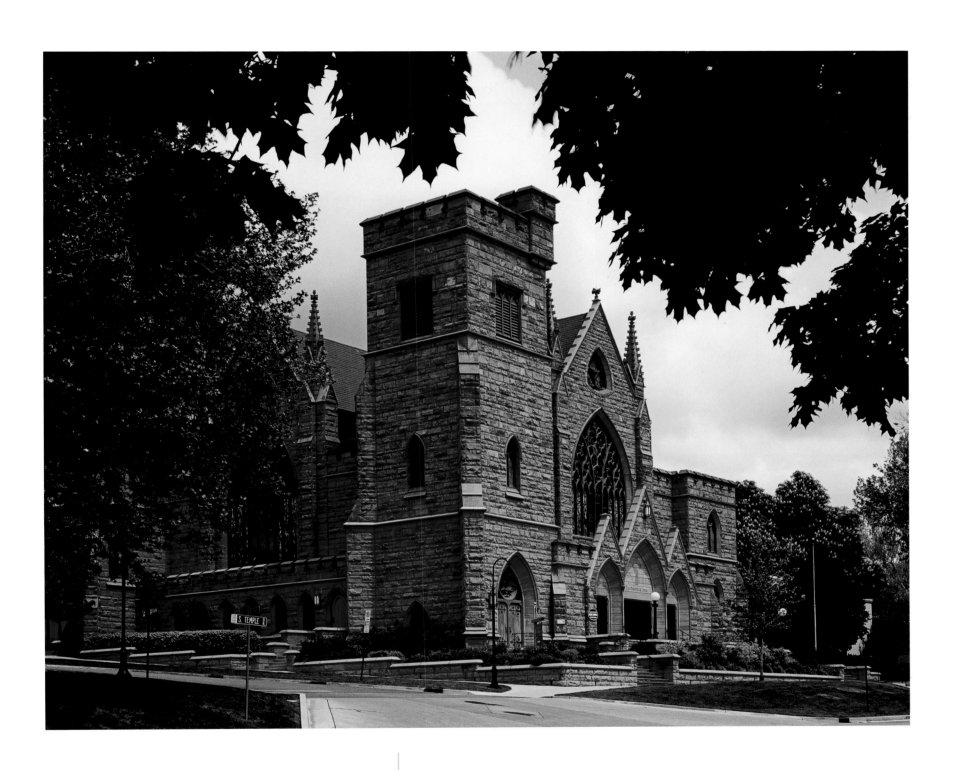

▲ Salt Lake City's First
Presbyterian Church
was modeled after the
English-Scottish Gothic
style of England's Carlisle
Cathedral.

◄ Statue titled The American Family graces the lawn of the historic Utah County Courthouse built with a neoclassical design in Provo.

► State Street stretches beyond the Utah State Capitol Building overlooking Salt Lake City.

Just a few miles east of the urban bustle of the Wasatch Front, alpine wildflowers flourish: ◄▲ Yellow columbine blooming from a crack in granite; ▲ Fireweed in the Bear River Range; ◄◄ Showy fleabane on flank of Mount Timpanogos; ◄ Paintbrush and Jacob's ladder in Maybird Gulch. ► Pond on the campus of Brigham Young University with Y Mountain beyond, Provo.

SOUTHWEST

▲ Thor's Hammer basking
in reflected light of
sunrise, Bryce Canyon
National Park.
► Bryce Amphitheater with
legions of Claron Formation
limestone hoodoos, Bryce
Canyon National Park.

◄ Entrada Formation white hoodoo, Grand
Staircase–Escalante National Monument.
▲ Along Wahweap Creek, a harder cap of
Dakota Sandstone protects softer white
badlands of the Entrada Formation.

◄ Joshua trees, a key species of the Mojave Desert, occur in the Beaver Dam Mountains in southwestern Utah.

▲ The Joshua Tree National Landmark has many fine specimens of this tree-forming yucca.

► Nearby Snow Canyon State Park has beautiful examples of Utah agave.

◄ The sun rising
through a narrow cloud
opening paints Agua
Canyon fiery red, Bryce
Canyon National Park.
► During winter's cold,
huge icicles cling to
the ceiling of Mossy
Cave, Bryce Canyon
National Park.

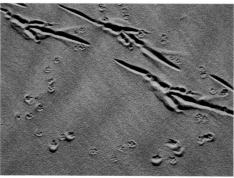

◄ Visitors gaze at Douglas fir growing between towering walls of Wall Street, Bryce Canyon National Park.
▲▲ Rain-soaked raven feather on Claron Formation limestone.
▲ Raven and mouse tracks on sand of Coral Pink Sand Dunes State Park.
► Boulder in Willis Creek Slot, Grand Staircase–Escalante National Monument below Bryce Canyon.

◄ Calf Creek Falls, Grand
Staircase–Escalante National
Monument.
▲▲ Navajo Sandstone
concretions or moqui marbles,
Snow Canyon State Park.
▲ Collared lizard basking in
sun, King Mesa, Glen Canyon
National Recreation Area.
► Paper-thin fins of wind-
eroded Navajo Sandstone,
Paria Canyon–Vermilion
Cliffs Wilderness.

► View from Point Supreme of hoodoos eroding from the Claron Formation, Cedar Breaks National Monument.

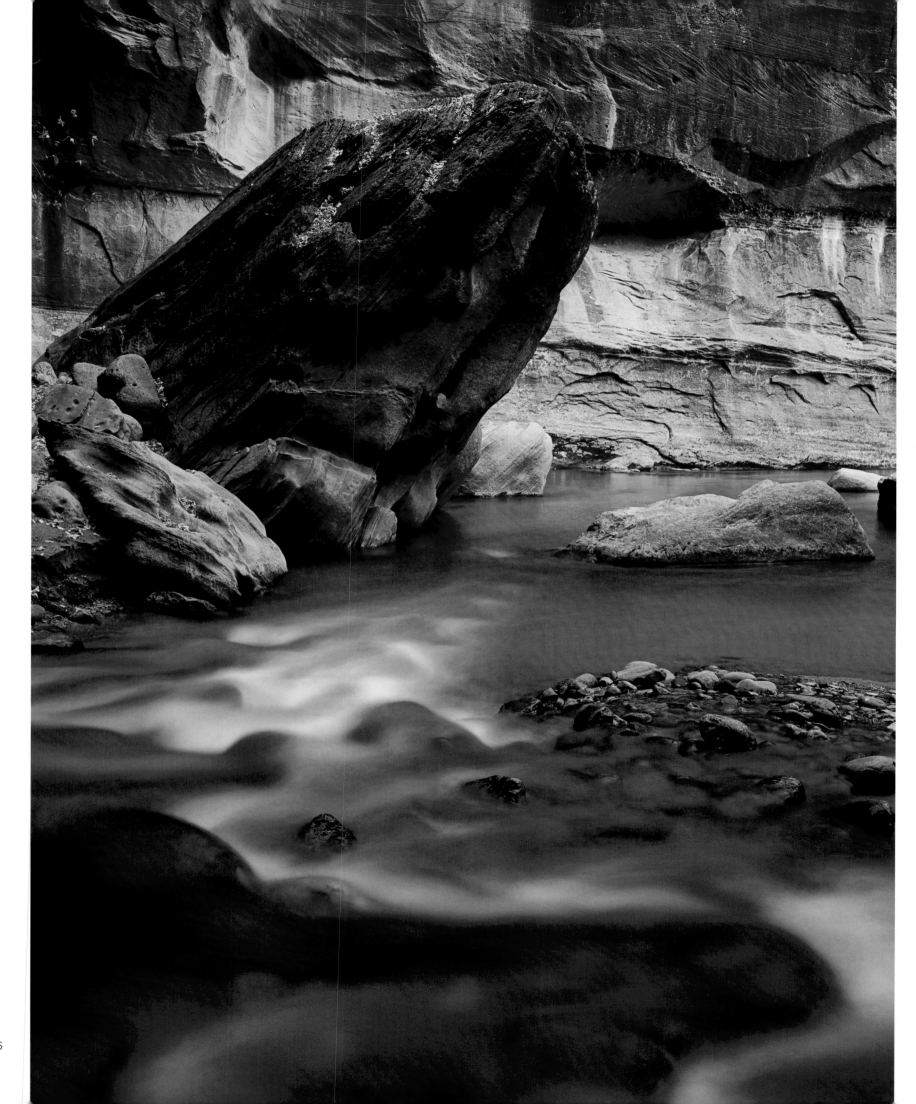

◄ North Fork Virgin River flowing through deep
confines of the Zion Narrows, Zion National Park.
▲ Box elders lining the canyon bottom of boulder-
strewn Clear Creek, Zion National Park.

▲ Dusting of early winter snow in Jericho Canyon,
Cedar Breaks National Monument.
▶ Ancient bristlecone pine in harsh environment
of Powell Point, Table Cliffs, Dixie National Forest.

▲ Gnarled juniper skeleton,
Hackberry Canyon, Grand
Staircase–Escalante National
Monument.
► Pinyon-juniper forest
leading toward sand
pipe and erosional
forms, Kodachrome
Basin State Park.

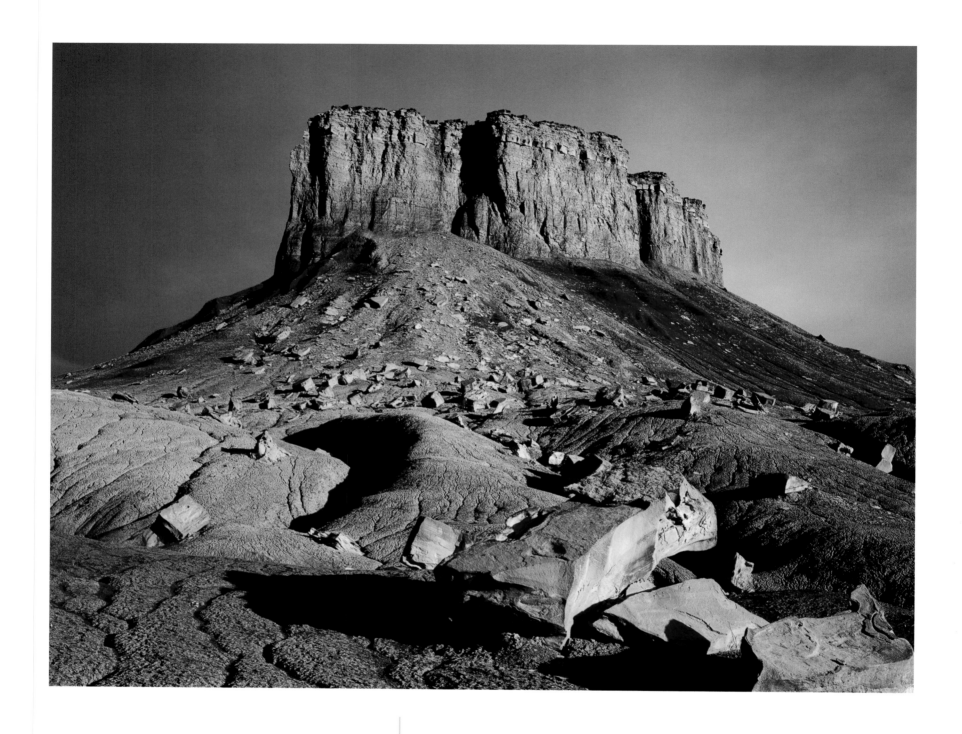

▲ Butte of Straight Cliffs
Formation sandstone capping
slopes of Tropic Shale near the
Rimrocks, Grand Staircase–
Escalante National Monument.
► Hard Dakota Sandstone
capping soft pillars of Entrada
Sandstone at the Toadstools,
Grand Staircase–Escalante
National Monument.

◄ Reds of bigtooth maple and yellows of Fremont cottonwood and canyon grape with sandstone monolith The Organ beyond, Zion National Park.

► Yellow bough of bigtooth maple along sandy bottom of Clear Creek, Zion National Park.

▶ Whitni Syrett with her horse, Chubs, in the small ranching community of Tropic.

▼ Cattle drive along the Cottonwood Canyon Road, Kane County.

▶▶ Two Feathers Ranch along the Virgin River with Eagle Crags of the Vermilion Cliffs beyond, Rockville.

◄ Wind-deposited sand thousands of feet thick created the Navajo Sandstone Formation so prominent in Utah. ► In the Paria Canyon–Vermilion Cliffs Wilderness, Navajo Sandstone erodes into myriad forms.

◄ Relatively soft limestone of the Claron Formation erodes into iron-stained hoodoos at Agua Canyon, Bryce Canyon National Park.
► Pink Cliffs of the Paunsaugunt Plateau erode two to four feet per century, exposing fanciful outcrops like the Poodle.
▼ Beneath the Bryce Canyon rim, a trail winds between fanciful hoodoos.

◄ Utah junipers in the
high desert of Hamlin
Valley near the Nevada
border in western Utah.
▲ Full moon rising
over Basin and Range
topography of
Swasey Mountain in
the House Range.

◄ Crystalline water of the Left Fork of North Creek filling potholes within the Subway, Zion National Park.

►▲ California sister butterfly collecting nectar from rubber rabbitbrush at Riggs Spring, Bryce Canyon National Park.

►►▲ Canyon tree frog beside Left Fork of North Creek, Zion National Park.

► Netted veins of last year's Fremont cotton-wood leaf, Davis Gulch, Glen Canyon National Recreation Area.

►► Claret cup hedgehog cactus in spring bloom, Zion National Park.

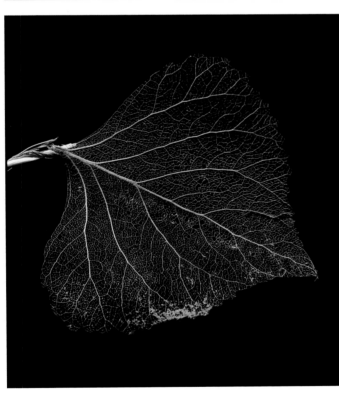

▲ Entrada Sandstone spires at
Kodachrome Basin State Park.
▶ Narrow-leaf cottonwoods
along the East Fork Sevier
River in Kingston Canyon,
Sevier Plateau, Piute County.

◄ Granite spires of
Sawtooth Mountain
rise from Tule Valley
at Painter Spring,
House Range.
► Lenticular clouds
gather above Nagunt
Mesa, Finger Canyons
of the Kolob, Zion
National Park.

◄ More durable magnesium-rich dolomite caps a formation called The Alligator below Bryce Point, Bryce Canyon National Park.

► Across Southern Utah, the Entrada Sandstone erodes into fanciful forms such as Metate Arch, Devil's Playground, Grand Staircase–Escalante National Monument.

◄ Fremont cottonwoods
and bluffs near Cannonville.
▲ Desert varnish coloring
Navajo Sandstone wall
behind blooming yucca in
Hackberry Canyon, Grand
Staircase–Escalante National
Monument.

◄ Ballard Home in ghost town of Grafton, originally settled as part of Brigham Young's Utah's Dixie cotton-growing project.

▲ Interior bedroom in Jacob Hamblin's Santa Clara home.

► Spinning wheel and loom upstairs in Hamblin's home.

►► Dining table and cupboard downstairs in Hamblin's home. Hamblin served as a missionary for the Latter-day Saints and diplomat to Native Americans in Utah and Arizona.

SOUTHEAST

▲ Fisher Towers, Cutler
Formation erosional spires
capped with harder
Moenkopi Sandstone.
► Wingate Sandstone cliffs and
Chinle Formation slopes at the
north end of King Bench, Circle
Cliffs, Grand Staircase–
Escalante National Monument.

◄ Utah juniper on rim of Elephant Canyon, Needles District, Canyonlands National Park.

► Gnarled Utah juniper and Mormon tea growing from Navajo Sandstone slickrock, Egypt, Glen Canyon National Recreation Area.

►► Gatefold: Chesler Park at sunset, Needles District, Canyonlands National Park.

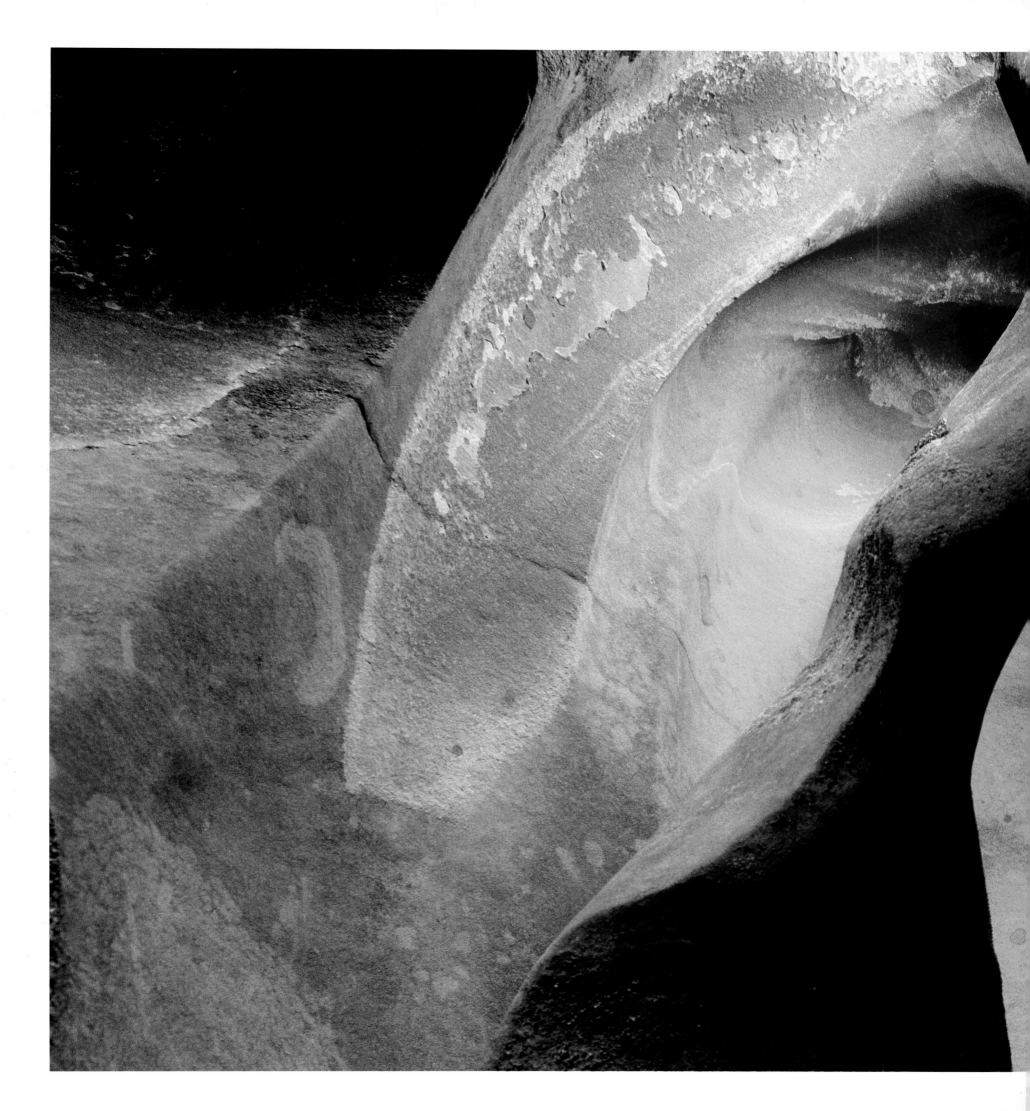

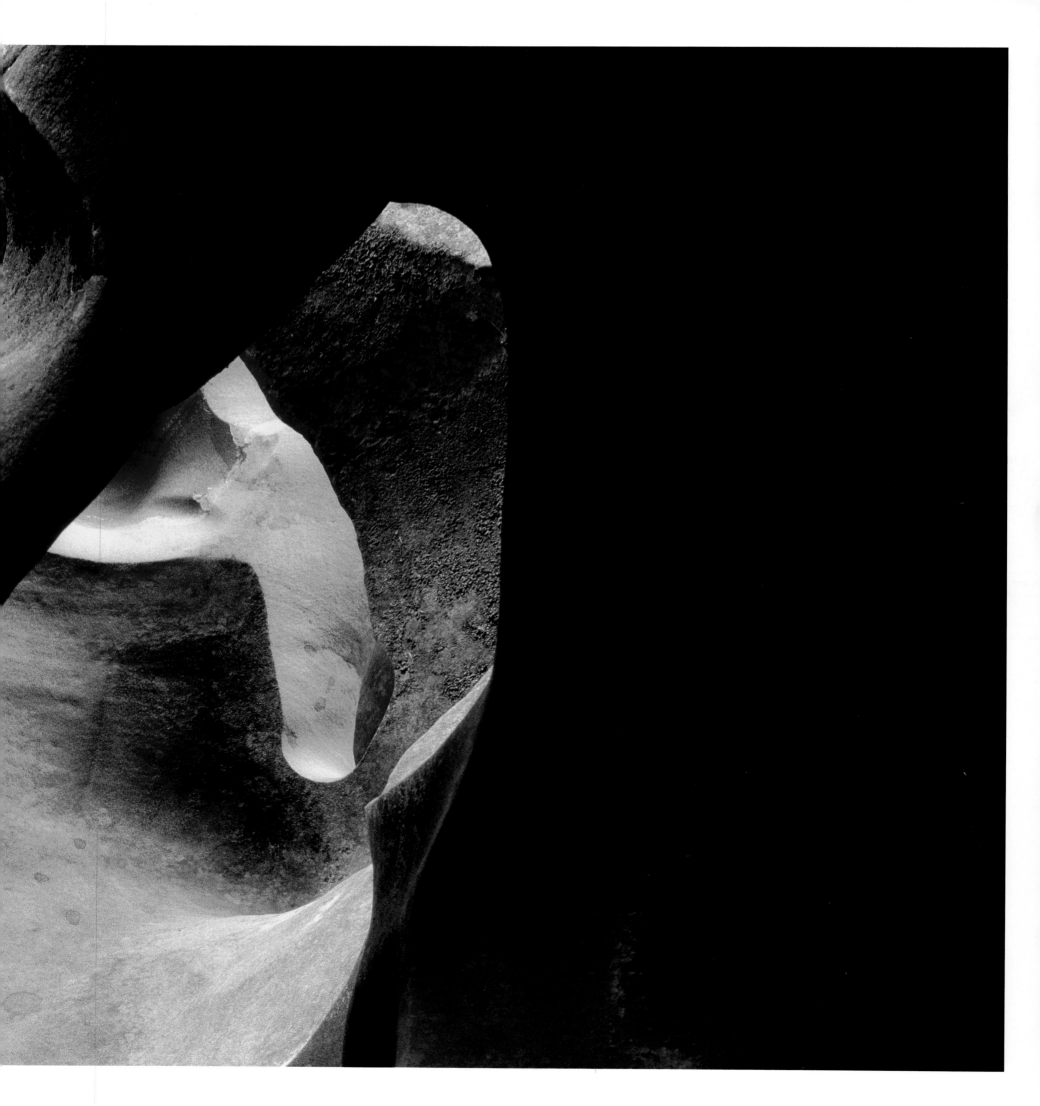

◄ Pothole Arch within a slot canyon, King Mesa, Grand Staircase–Escalante National Monument.

► White badlands of Entrada Formation mudstone near Wahweap Creek, Grand Staircase–Escalante National Monument.

◄ Cracking pattern of drying mud decorates slot canyon floor, Grand Staircase–Escalante National Monument.

► Sinuous passageway a few feet wide, but dozens of feet deep, carved by flash floods in Navajo Sandstone.

▲ Ice adhering to boulders
in Negro Bill Canyon,
Colorado Riverway east
of Moab.
► Winter snow accents
Sitting Hen Butte, Valley
of the Gods.

▲ Crystal Arch in
the backcountry of
Arches National Park.
▶ Dusting of winter
snow on the Goosenecks
of the San Juan,
Goosenecks State Park.

◄ Fluted carving of Coyote Wash as it cuts through Navajo Sandstone, Coyote Gulch, Glen Canyon National Recreation Area.
► Sun shining on Fremont cottonwood growing between towering walls of Coyote Gulch, Glen Canyon National Recreation Area.

◄ Appropriately named
Parade of Elephants is but
one of an estimated two
thousand natural stone arches
in Arches National Park.
▲ Bulrushes grow through
last year's cottonwood leaf,
riparian tributary of the
Escalante River, Glen Canyon
National Recreation Area.

◄◄ Pictographs of eight intaglio handprints on wall of sandstone shelter above Indian Creek.

▲ Jailhouse Ruin, Ancestral Puebloan site in Bullet Canyon, Grand Gulch Primitive Area.

◄ Mud spiral pictograph on soot-covered wall at Green Mask Spring, Grand Gulch Primitive Area.

► Dusk light on Hovenweep Castle, Ancestral Puebloan dwelling on edge of Little Ruin Canyon, Hovenweep National Monument.

◄ Sunset illuminates virga
falling above slickrock of
Arches National Park.
▲ Reflected sunlight
casts an orange glow
in narrow passageway
between sandstone fins
of Fiery Furnace, Arches
National Park.

◄ Airport Tower looms above the White Rim, Island in the Sky District of Canyonlands National Park.
▼ Double Arch, a pothole arch formed by water erosion from above, is the third-largest span in Arches National Park.

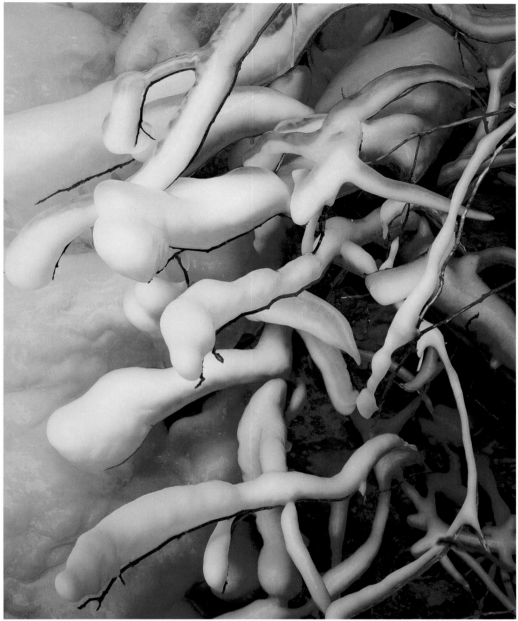

◄ Pan ice threatens to
freeze across the
Colorado River along
Arches National Park.
▲ Ice coats branches
below a slickrock
canyon waterfall,
Colorado Riverway.
► Fremont cottonwood
leaf on ice, Horseshoe
Canyon, Canyonlands
National Park.

▲ Spires of red and white layered sandstone
typify Cedar Mesa Sandstone in Chesler Park,
Needles District of Canyonlands National Park.
▶ The North Window frames Turret Arch in
winter, Arches National Park.

▲ Keyhole entrance of
Ancestral Puebloan living
quarters, Cedar Mesa.
▶ Painted stucco
covering an amazingly
well-preserved Ancestral
Puebloan dwelling,
Cedar Mesa.

◄ Colorado River viewed from the Gooseneck Overlook, White Rim Trail, Canyonlands National Park.
► Fremont cottonwood in autumn splendor, Labyrinth Canyon of the Green River.

▼ Hickman Natural Bridge, with an opening 125 feet high and 133 feet across, Capitol Reef National Park.
▶ On canyon wall of Buckhorn Wash, the rust-red pigments of Barrier Canyon pictographs may be 1,500 to 3,000 years old, San Rafael Swell.

◄ Green joint fir or
Mormon tea, mountain
pepperbush, and Utah
juniper snag, Capitol
Reef National Park.
▲▲ Common raven,
Canyonlands
National Park.
▲ Paintbrush and sand
sagebrush, Willow Gulch,
Glen Canyon National
Recreation Area.
► Dwarf aster, Capitol
Reef National Park.

▲ Ice waterfall, Colorado
Riverway in winter.
► Winter dawn in
Valley of the Gods,
San Juan County.

◄ Exquisite contemporary
Navajo baskets woven by
Elsie Holiday, Peggy Black,
Fannie King, Alicia Nelson,
and Mary Black, Twin
Rocks Trading Post, Bluff.
► Boulder-strewn narrows
of Wetherill Canyon,
Navajo Reservation south
of Lake Powell.

◄ Rainbow Bridge, the world's largest natural bridge with an opening 290 feet tall and 275 feet wide, Rainbow Bridge National Monument.

► Sipapu Natural Bridge with a height of 220 feet and a span of 268 feet, Natural Bridges National Monument.

◄ Long after a flash flood roared downstream, pools remain in White Canyon.

► Aerial view of Candlestick Tower with Island in the Sky beyond, Canyonlands National Park.

◄ Green River flowing through Upheaval Bottom, Labyrinth Canyon, Canyonlands National Park.

▲ Birchleaf buckthorn growing from a crack in Navajo Sandstone, Davis Gulch, Glen Canyon National Recreation Area.

◄ Aerial view of Mancos Formation badlands south of North Caineville Mesa.
► Ferron Sandstone caps soft Mancos Shale at Factory Butte northwest of Hanksville.

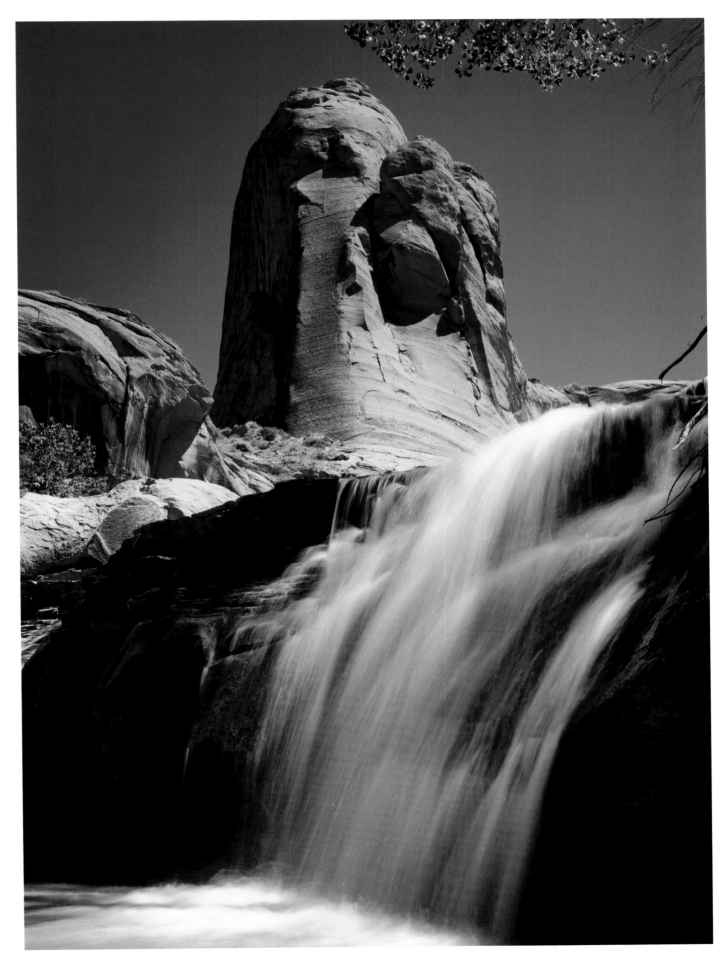

◄ Balanced rock, a large boulder of Wingate Sandstone protects a soft pillar of Chinle Formation mudstone, Wolverine Bench, Grand Staircase–Escalante National Monument.

► Waterfall in Coyote Gulch, Escalante River tributary, Glen Canyon National Recreation Area.

◄ Erosional pattern
in sandstone wall of
Fremont Canyon, Capitol
Reef National Park.
► Utah juniper on
low reef east of the
Waterpocket Fold, Capitol
Reef National Park.

◄ Orange glowing
chamber inside a slickrock
slot canyon, Grand
Staircase–Escalante
National Monument.
► Peek-a-Boo Arch
on the crest of the
Waterpocket Fold near
Upper Muley Twist
Canyon, Capitol Reef
National Park.

◄ Autumn gold of
quaking aspen along
Mill Creek, western
slope of the La Sal
Mountains, Manti–La Sal
National Forest.
► Aspen trunks below
Miners Basin, La Sal
Mountains, Manti–La Sal
National Forest.

Library of Congress Control Number: 2008930587
International Standard Book Number: 978-0-88240-745-6

President: Charles M. Hopkins
Associate Publisher: Douglas A. Pfeiffer
Editorial Staff: Tim Frew, Kathy Howard, Jean Bond-Slaughter
Production Staff: Heather Doornink, Susan Dupèré
Designers: Elizabeth Watson, Jean Andrews
Prepress color: Fred Hirschmann, Haagen Printing
Printer: Haagen Printing
Binding: Lincoln & Allen Co.

Book compilation © MMVIII by Graphic Arts™ Books
An imprint of Graphic Arts Center Publishing Company
P.O. Box 10306, Portland, Oregon 97296-0306
503/226-2402; www.gacpc.com

Printed and bound in the United States of America

Page 1 Escalante River tributary within Glen Canyon National Recreation Area.
Page 2 Claron Formation hoodoos, Agua Canyon, Bryce Canyon National Park.
Page 3 Douglas firs reaching for the sky, Wall Street, Bryce Canyon National Park.
Pages 4–5 Delicate Arch with La Sal Mountains beyond, Arches National Park.
Page 5 (Northwest) Playa and Deep Creek Range.
Page 5 (Northeast) Morrison Formation badlands, Green River, Dinosaur National Monument.
Page 5 (Wasatch) Aspen framing Mount Timpanogos, Wasatch Range.
Page 5 (Southwest) Navajo Sandstone beehive, Paria Canyon–Vermilion Cliffs Wilderness.
Page 5 (Southeast) North Window framing Turret Arch, Arches National Park.
Page 202 Sun backlighting hoodoo above the Peek-a-Boo Trail, Bryce Canyon National Park.
Page 203 Fifteen inches of fresh snow on the floor of Zion Canyon, Zion National Park.

◄ Archangel Cascades, Left Fork of North Creek, Zion National Park.

► Intricately eroded sandstone of the Uinta Formation, Fantasy Canyon.

►► (pages 200–201) Sunrise along the east end of the Towers of the Virgin following a winter storm, Zion National Park.

►►► (page 204) Red glow from the aurora during a geomagnetic storm and star trails circling Polaris during a three-hour exposure, Wolverine Bench.

PHOTO NOTES

When I mentioned to fellow landscape photographer and friend Jeff Gnass that I was working on a new Utah photo-essay book, Jeff responded that I would be photographing what was already the most photographed state in the union! With Utah's incredible collection of national parks, monuments, forests, wilderness areas, and state parks, drawing an estimated 17.5 million visitors annually, Jeff likely was right. People take plenty of pictures of Utah's sublime splendors.

But Jeff's implication that all of Utah's pictures might already have been taken didn't bother me a bit for I knew from all my explorations that Utah held hundreds— no, thousands—of seldom-visited and little-known gems.

The icons of the state, say Delicate Arch in Arches National Park, see hoards of photographers daily. For any given sunset, there may be twenty to fifty folks gathered along the slickrock bowl leading to this famous arch, tripods lined up like a digital firing squad. Woe be to the wayward individual with pocket camera who wanders into everybody else's picture! To keep the peace, the park service has even developed arch etiquette requesting folks not be "arch hogs" by hanging out inside the arch and down-range of the photo firing line.

Most people miss that the 76,519 acres of Arches National Park hold an additional two thousand other arches and many of these natural rock openings often go weeks or years between human visits. The park trail winding

through the Devil's Garden passes many exquisite arches with quiet and solitude just about guaranteed.

In the past three decades, a plethora of hiking guides have been published on routes through Utah's mountains and canyons. A common theme of the authors seems to be prerequisite snapshots of the alpine lakes, canyon narrows, and perhaps a settler's cabin or Indian ruin seen along the way. The text almost always mentions how quickly the author accomplished the hike, covering maybe twelve or fifteen miles in four or five hours.

To get good photographs, my number one rule is to slow down. Being in the backcountry doesn't mean you have to travel the trails like you were racing on I-15 between St. George and Salt Lake in an afternoon! Of course, carrying thirty to forty-five pounds of camera gear slows me down. But the leisurely pace provides time to intimately study the landscape. I'll see the natural beauty in the whorl of a Utah agave's leaves or the erosional pattern of cross-bedded Navajo Sandstone.

And hiking at a slower pace allows me a greater opportunity to be out for that moment of magical light surrounding the hours of sunrise or sunset or at the breaking of a storm. In areas that allow overnight camping, I often carry a sleeping bag so I may spend time in the area waiting for that perfect light.

As I travel, I also study the landscape, preconceptualizing how the light may illuminate a given subject at a certain time of day. Perhaps I'll see a hanging garden of maidenhair ferns that appears too contrasty in midday sun, but will photograph beautifully after the ferns pass into shade and are softly lit by warm light bouncing off an adjacent canyon wall.

In recent years, a common refrain of people viewing my photography has been, "Oh, those pictures look nice, they must be digital." To which I smile and reply, "Nope, I'm a Luddite. They are all taken on film." The technology I favor most was developed in the latter half of the nineteenth century, not created in our current first part of the twenty-first century. With movable bellows, camera manufacturers of old learned how to optimize sharpness by allowing tilting of the camera lens to greatly increase depth of field. To correct for perspective distortion, the lens was allowed to rise and shift. Proper positioning of the lens may take time, but the results on a 4x5-inch transparency can be stunningly beautiful.

In the book you are holding, of the 238 photographic plates, 167—or more than two-thirds—were taken with a large-format Toyo 45 All Field Camera. The Toyo 4x5-inch camera always sits on an Arca-Swiss Monoball attached to a sturdy Gitzo tripod, and here I do enjoy the modern technology of carbon fiber, which shaves about two pounds off the weight of older aluminum tripods. Composing and focusing of images is performed under a dark cloth on a glass plate. Metering is done with a tried-and-true Pentax Spotmeter V. I typically carry twenty film holders in the field, which allow me to shoot forty sheets of film before I need to set up a portable changing bag and reload fresh film. After a full day of shooting, I need one to two hours to clean dust from holders and change film. For hard-core camera buffs, my favorite lenses on the 4x5 are a 75mm f4.5 Nikkor-SW, 120mm f5.6 Schneider Super-Symmar HM, 180mm f5.6 Rodenstock Apo-Sironar-S, 210mm f5.6 Fujinon-W, 300mm f9 Nikkor-M and Nikkor-T 360mm/500mm. Most images are shot at tiny apertures between f32 and f45 that allow for precise sharpness and long exposure times typically ranging from one-eighth of a second for midday shots to two to six minutes for images taken in the pale light of dusk and dawn. On windy days, I've been known to wait hours for a flower to quit bouncing.

For the wildlife and people shots and some of the landscapes you see in the book, sixty-four plates were taken with medium-format Pentax 645N and Mamiya 645 cameras using 120mm roll film. Again, a tripod was almost always underfoot, and for longer exposures, the

camera's mirror was raised to keep mirror bounce from blurring an image. I used Pentax SMC-FA 45mm, 75mm, 210mm, and 400mm lenses and Mamiya Sekor 45mm, 80mm, 120mm Macro, and 500mm lenses.

Five of the images appearing in the book were taken with my trusty thirty-five-year-old Pentax Spotmatic screw mount camera. For shooting straight into the sun without any perceptible lens flaring, nothing beats this camera's 28mm f3.5 Super Takumar lens. If you find one on eBay, buy it. Just don't burn out your retina staring at the sun!

With the exception of a polarizing filter, which I use sparingly, and a center spot filter that evens the exposure on the Nikkor-SW 75mm lens, no filters have been used on any of my images. My film of choice for both medium and large format is Fuji's Velvia 50 and 100 and Kodak's Ektachrome 100VS.

Shooting more than one thousand sheets of 4x5 film and a couple hundred rolls of 120 in a month keeps the E6 line at the photo lab busy. Film for this Utah book was developed

in Denver, at Qube Visual and more recently in Boulder at Photo-Craft Imaging. All scanning of the transparencies was done on our Hasselblad Imacon 848 and 949 virtual drum scanners, which do a wonderful job of capturing the detail, sharpness, and colors of the transparencies and translating this information into large digital files. I like telling folks that shooting 4x5-inch transparencies and scanning the images with the Hasselblad Imacons is like having a 150-megapixel camera!

Most of the credit for a book like this rightfully goes to the incredible beauty of nature. There is a human element, too. In that, I would like to thank the unwavering support of my wife, Randi, who joined me on some photo trips and patiently ran the office all too often when I was in the field.

Friends who shared in Utah adventures include Tim Pfieffer, Scott Thybony, Jennifer Whipple, and the late Rick Hutchinson. Larry Van Slyke, pilot extraordinaire, provided an aerial shooting platform in friend Clair Roberts's trusty Cessna 170B. Alta skiers Dylan Crossman and Brittany Lewis shepherded me through their totally awesome freestyle skiing. Debbie Westfall, Curator at Edge of the Cedars State Park Museum, trusted me with photographing some of the most exquisite Ancestral Puebloan pottery in any collection. Steve Simpson at Twin Rocks Trading Post let me photograph the wonderful contemporary Navajo baskets created by local weavers. To these people, and those unmentioned, I owe my heartfelt gratitude.

—FRED HIRSCHMANN